AF430279

To my poet-artist.

Seasonal Happiness

No Way Out

No winter lasts forever
but this one seems to never end
Cold rain
on my frozen skin
Music to warm my heart
Thoughts darker
than the night sky
Soft lights that
hurt my eyes
The desire of happiness
and the desire to escape
from this place
from myself
from my life
But there's
no way out
because this winter never ends.

The child is afraid

Sobbing violently
on the rain and the piano
so soft and broken
the night leaves you
breathless

And in its
pitch black
darkness
you drown in
your pain

Lake

The only thing that's real
is the ache in my chest
and every painful breath
stings like tears that
won't be cried

Is this my last writing?
Perhaps
Perhaps

Perhaps you'll find me
and realize that
there was nothing beautiful
in me

It was your reflection
all along

Snowflake in a hoodie

Oh, the comfort of
a hoodie
hiding what you want
to love,
so desperately
but you cannot
because if you
don't hate
that soft landscape
its beauty
its strength
you can't call yourself
You

She – Dead (name)

The person that answers to
that name
isn't me
it's her
everything you wanted
her to be
something they long for,
sometimes
someone they'll never be
again

You're killing someone
who's alive
calling for a ghost
that lives in memories,
in everyone's minds
but theirs.

Set her free,
don't call that name
ever again.

Let the dead go,
let the river flow.

Flesh (prison)

I want to love you
as me
not as her
I want my scars
to touch your heart
I want your hands
on my curves
I want to say your name
with a voice that feels
like mine

I want your sun
on my skin
Melt my wings
and set me free
in your embrace

I am you / you are me

Don't run
from me
Don't try
to fight me
You need me
You know
you need me

Let me in
I'll be gentle
Feed me
let me feast
on the shadows
your mind casts

Don't be scared
you know me,
don't you?
We are friends

I am you

And you are
me

You can
let the light in
but when you
look in the mirror
you know
you can't drown
me out

Poor little thing,
you're a crumpled up
piece of paper
now, lying
on the bathroom
floor
and I am
the hand
that crushed
you

Grey like death

I feel like
an empty thing
that was once
a piece of art
so beautiful
and full of life

Now I'm just
a broken vase
They took all
my flowers
and my bees,
my precious little
friends
are crying

But no one
mourns and weeps
for me

lonely / lost

Coming home
to no one
it's not even
a place
I can call
home

I'm just
a lost piece
of nothing
floating
in the universe,
no purpose
no destination
only pain

snowflakes / selene

You should have been here.

And now
no matter
how far
I stretch
my arm out
I can't reach you

How many times
snowflakes
will fall
on my eyes
before I can
see you
again?

As the days
pass by
I'm so full
of grief,
I don't know
where
to put it

Weeping Willow

Take me where
the mountains are green
and the grass
looks soft like
your big tender hands

Lay down with me
and let's watch the
clouds
grey and free
in a way I could never
be

Let me crave

the snow on top
and the horizon
that keeps me
from leaving my roots

And then let go
of my body
that you love holding
so close
to your heartbeat

Sing to me
while I drown
with my eyes open
in the cold lake

I want to be

I want to be
the snowy wind
and slide
in your t-shirt,
caressing your neck
and arms,
making you shiver,
to remind you
how warm you are.

I want to be
the stars at night
and make
your sweet eyes
sparkle,
to reassure you
that there's always light
even when you can't
see it.

I want to be
the sun during spring
and kiss
your precious skin,
to show you
that you'll never be cold
and a new beginning
will always find you.

I want to be
the quiet rain
and wash
away your pain,
hugging your tears
and your body,
to lift
some weight off your
chest
and breathe
more easily.

My sun

Stars on my arms
and stars in your eyes
because you are
the light of my life
and you flow through
my veins

Forever

What if
I don't get
another life
to love you?

What if
after all
this pain
I'll come into
another life
and I am
just the same?

What if
you're not
there
and I am
alone, again

Forever

Rough

My hands
were softer
when they could
touch your face

I was softer,
too

(Post) Love Letter

Promises are
meant to be
broken
I know that,
I know
but I gave you
a promise ring
anyway
and now
it sits in
the pink box,
waiting to be
forgotten

I'm trying
to forget
the spark
in your blue eyes
the warmth
of your arms
the words
you said and meant
But they never
quite matched

your actions

And I'm not
shitting on
what we once
called us
It was good
it was tender
it was perfect
it was precious
it was great,
even when
it wasn't
when I wasn't
when you,
yes you
you weren't

Now I let
our songs
fade into
background noise
the poetry
is still there
but the spark

is gone
Because you
let me down
your selfishness
poisoned my heart
and stained
our memories,
painted them
with a darker
colour

But the sun
shines
on my beloved
snowy mountains
and the anger
won't last forever
and I'm writing you
a post-love letter
because
time eases
the ache,
but
I can't forget you

I still love you

March (in the rain)

You left me
alone
in the rain
for five long months
and when
I found
the sun again
you cried
that your flowers
are dying

Who will
take care
of my soil,
now?

I cannot be
your blue sky
your sun
your rain
the gentle wind
that guides
your petals,

not anymore

Not after
you gave me
just enough
warmth
for my drenched
land
not to drown
and
took my thorns
one by one
until my skin
was bare
and tender

Do you like
the taste
of blood?
The same
taste that
keeps me
awake at
night,

while I watch
the stars die
and the moon
hides and
weeps
for her child

Bleed, kid
you know
that first love
never lasts

Dream of me, I'll dream of you

You say
our paths
will cross again
but I
don't believe
in falling stars
and red strings
anymore

And you used
to say
dream of me
so I did
but even
in my dreams
you didn't
love me
the same
anymore

Do you ever

dream of me,
too?
And if you do,
do you embrace me
and kiss my forehead?
Do you smile
and laugh with me?
Or do you watch my
back
as you grab my hips?

When I
close my eyes
I see your face
and I
want to cry
but when
you close
your eyes
you only see
the night

plastic plant / the doll

Let me
show some skin,
put on a dress
or a skirt,
perhaps
Let me
fix my eyeliner,
wear a sparkly,
thin bracelet
Let me
adjust my mask
over this pretty face
And maybe,
maybe you'll stay
maybe you'll love me
forever

Let me
swallow harsh words,
tell you I'm okay
Let me
cancel that
appointment,
get better grades

Let me
pretend to forget
that you never
apologize
to me
And maybe,
maybe you won't walk
away
maybe you'll play the
role
just for a while

Let me
paint a smile
over these scars
Let me
say yes
yes, yes, yes
do you need
something?
can I help you?
don't worry about me
no need to thank me
sorry, I'm so sorry

sorry, sorry, sorry
Let me
change
every little thing
about myself
until I'm
someone else
until I'm
like everyone else
And maybe,
just maybe
I'll be perfect,
unbroken
and empty,
colourless
No reflection
to claim
No pain
to feel
No growth
for a plastic plant

The angry man

I don't think
you're bad
you're always
working hard
to put a smile
on my face
but when I smile,
oh how I wish
I could say
it's because of you

I will smile
I will not
scream in your face
like you often do
I will bite back
so many words
those words you
don't understand

I will laugh
while I tell others
how hopeless
I feel, sometimes

their concern
will not reach
me

And I will cry
in the silence
of this place
away from you
I will pick
myself up,
look in the mirror
and see
the angry man's
face
stained with tears

Funny, isn't it?

Her eyes,
your anger
what do they make?
An imperfect creature,
split in two

Sorry I cannot
be like you

Father, I am a rich man / heart made of gold

You judge
my lovers
by their bank account
by the colours
that flow
in their veins
You don't even
know half of them

Her, she was
a different kind
of first love
I was
a kid
but the butterflies
were the same

And her,
the definition
of right person,
wrong time

Do you remember

that big, red package?
From them, "just
a friend"
Broke my heart,
but the pain
was sublime

Him, you actually
know him
never thought badly
of him,
because all you saw
was his wealth
All I saw
was someone
who didn't even
exist
I created him

You will never know
what he did
to me

Is this
what you hope for?
For me
to marry a wealthy man

Father,
I am a rich man
but you refuse
to see
the man
and the richness inside
those emotions
that make you scoff
but they're
the most precious thing
I own

This heart
is made
of gold

Family / inner child

Father,
tell me
this gift
of yours
where can I
put it
when I don't
need it
anymore
when I don't
want it
anymore?

Your anger
has kept me
alive
for enough time,
now
I think my fire
has been fed
enough
and it can
survive
on its own

Mother,
tell me
this void
you left me
will it always
be painful
to look at
to touch?

Your absence
has taught me
to love everyone
but myself
and yet
the seed
I planted
is timidly growing

Sister,
tell me
what is it like
to have a brother
are you

ashamed
of me?

If you are
you hide it
so well,
now

Come, child
we're safe
I've got
hugs for you
and tissues
to wipe
your tears
and ears
to listen
to your pain

Baby,
I'm sorry
I'm so sorry
you don't have
to forgive them
but forgive
yourself
forgive me
for the mistakes
I still make

And one day,
I hope
you'll be
proud of me
just like I am
proud of you

Free me

He has the sweetest eyes
I've ever seen
He doesn't talk much
But they do
And they smile
And the flowers sing
While the snowflakes
dance
On his pretty eyelashes

I'm so cold
When our bones are
apart
He's red like blood
When my gaze finally

Finds him in the crowd

He's silent
And I'm a ghost
A crying summer
thunderstorm

I haunt him
like loneliness haunts
my bed

Free me
Free me
Free me
Free me

Wolf

I never sleep enough
Always up thinking
About your sweet face
While my heart pumps
pain
While my eyes pour
Wasted love

Wasted words
You ignore
With that smile
That makes flowers
bloom

I cannot heal
Not yet
Not yet
Because your light
Is full of thorns

I'm a pitch black

Bleeding moon
I'm howling at myself
In my burning cold
messy head

Self-sabotage

We dress up
as villains
we play
our roles
for our own
entertainment
but when
we take off
the masks
your face is
angelic and pure
and I am
the bad guy

I'm holding
the dagger
so tight
blood drips
from my fingers

Run,
before I
lose control

It's okay
if I am
the one bleeding
but you have
to run
before I
start chasing
you

Run,
please
I can't tame
the monster

(You deserve better
This was
too good
for my wretched
soul, anyway)

I want you
to stay
but really,
you should

run away

(You can't
tame me)

IV

I became my own God
So I can ignore my
prayers
Let others worship me
And not worship them
back
Because I've forgotten
how to
Admire myself in the
mirror
And weep violently at
the sight

Why does a God
Have memories
Of you playing
With my rings
Your imperfectly crafted
Hands

Why does a God

Keep the memories
Of the crispy cold
December

Those days are so far
away now
Only the pain lingers
I can taste the snow
On my teeth
It tastes like yearning

Are you ashamed,
God?
You must be
Why would I silently
cry?
Does your heart ache,
God?
Another winter has
come

Roots

January

brings back memories
of my first heartbreak

Some days the air
tastes like home
and spring
I'm fourteen
and my hands have
never touched your
curls

A poet never forgets
their first muse

My love,
how I miss those days
your doe eyes
the eternal spring
my stupid innocence
the melody my soul
used to sing
for you

I'm almost twenty-one
My fingers are frozen
under this green sky
And the wind

Letter to my best friend

You're my world
and so
in my world
nothing goes unnoticed
not the streets,
not the stars,
not the tiny
new born flowers
not even
the dying grass
of November

And darling, you're
my love story
And the moon
is smiling
And it's
the most tender
caress
I've ever felt
And we're made
of words

You make me feel
like all the poets
in the world
are singing
for me,
and leading
my words
out there

And this is
the closest feeling
to being immortal

I am in love
in a way
I've never been
with other people:
the love of gods

I adore you
like one adores
cute little animals
and flowers
and the warmth
of the sun
before summer

and the peace
and immensity
of water,
of lakes
and seas
and oceans

Let's spark together
and when it gets
so dark,
we'll sing
to the moon

Phone call

The moon
kisses our faces
the same
the waves
carry our laughs
in their song

We met during
one painful summer
but to me,
my sweet angel,
you are spring
a blessing
in my messy life

You're tender
pink flowers

and you're
an old tree
strong and peaceful
in the storm
calm and smiling,
reassuring
in the breeze

You're poetry
that awaits
to be loved

And I am
a poet
blissfully
listening to
you

Eos

I am the night
and when we meet,
we dance softly, and you
paint me in your
colours,
and I can breathe,

And you kiss
my falling stars
one by one.

Lemon clouds

No one wants someone
else's heavy, overflowing
feelings
But I am a river
And so I will accept
your waves
Whether gentle or
violent
Every single cloud cries,
sooner or later
But if you keep moving
you'll always go on
Because even the
calmest river knows
the restlessness of the
storm

It's hard to forget you're
alive when you taste
lemon

There's always time to
build a new you
Sometimes from the
start
Sometimes from ruins
Under the clouds,
next to the river
you can do anything

So when life gives you lemons
Remember that there's oxygen
in your lungs
And it tastes bitter and yellow

Let it rain / a way out

The world is so ugly
sometimes you
fall on the hard,
cold ground
everything hurts
is it worth it?
Getting up,
trying again
asking yourself
the same old questions
and no answers
to be found

Let it hurt
Let it rain
Forget about the
answers

I will lie down

with you
I will embrace
your pain,
take it as my own
It can't rain forever
It won't rain forever
Even the coldest of
winters
doesn't last forever

And so I will
wait with you
until the ground
is warm
until flowers bloom
and you can take
my hand
and try again

And we fly

Never again,
I say
holding my poor heart
my devastated,
poor heart

Never again,
with my back
turned to
the cliff
I'm never,
ever
jumping again

Terrified
I am
of my soul
being crushed
from the fall

Never
Never
Never

Again

You look
at me
with those
genuine green
eyes of yours
you don't even
say please

And my heart
screams
yes again!
Again,
again,
again,
please

One more time
One more jump
One more fall

And we fly

Welcome home

Life is
so much better
than it was
I've got the sun
in my arms
my hair is short
and my smile
bigger than
my beloved mountains

I don't need
to go home
not anymore
because you're
here, shining
in my arms

And you're
warm
you're
alive
you're
soft
and fast
asleep
between
the lake
and
the stars
on my lap

Modern Love Letter

Can I have
the last apple?
Yes,
yes you can
it was
waiting for you

I open
the window
so you can
smoke
and while
you do,
I take
the coke
out of
the fridge

Can I borrow-
... my sweatpants?
... my t-shirt?
... my oxygen?
My darling,
you can

keep it
if it means
you exist
for one more
second

I wander
in every shop
and I
look for
a piece
of you
a plushie,
or
something spiky,
maybe
or
pencils
and markers
and highlighters

Can I stay
the night?
Oh love,

please stay
for the rest
of my life
(But if
you have
to leave
I hope
the wind
kisses your cheeks
and
the sun
never sleeps
so each step
you take
will be
in the light)

I play
Queen,

Mother Mother,
and even
that song
you despise,
just to
make you laugh
make you sing
make you dance
with me, clumsily

My robin,
so small
and soft
and fierce
blooming red,
your heart
You painted
the winter away
from my soul

March (in the sun)

The shadows
of the trees
painted on
the streets
make me
tear up

They're alive

The sun
kisses
the flowers
and they
smile at it
it kisses
my face
my hands
my heart

I'm alive

Warm
and loud
is my friends'

laughter
on the stairs,
in between
the courses
Warm
and pink
is the sunset
when my
shoulders
relax
against the wall
Warm
and sparkly
are your emerald green
eyes
while you lay
next to me
in the dry,
luscious grass
of March,
in the sun

You're alive

It's March
and my soul
muses about
the sunny days

THANKS TO

My readers, both old and new. Thank you for your support, your patience, your affection and enthusiasm which you show for every single one of my works, whether poetry or prose.

Thanks to my best friend, Leonard, who inspires me with his art.

Thanks to Aurora, my precious small flower and one of my biggest fans. Never stop shining, darling.

Thanks to J, my moon.

Thanks to Bunny, my sweet boyfriend and one of the reasons why I've been so inspired lately.